THIS BOOK BELONGS TO

_____

_____

PRESENTED BY

_____

DATE

FATIMA
Family Handbook
Heaven's Plan for Your Family

TOM HOOPES

Illustrations by Caroline Spinelli & Chris Pelicano

HOLY HEROES BOOKS · CRAMERTON, NORTH CAROLINA

HOLY HEROES FATIMA FAMILY HANDBOOK
Copyright ©2017 by Holy Heroes, LLC.
All rights reserved. No portion of this book may be reproduced in any form without the written permission of the publisher, with the exception of brief excerpts in reviews.

Text by Tom Hoopes
Illustrations by Caroline Spinelli and Chris Pelicano

Printed in the U.S.A.   ISBN 978-1-936330-74-4

To order more books visit **www.HolyHeroes.com**
or call **1-855-Try2B-Holy** (1-855-879-2246)

Table of Contents

"Our Lady needs you—all!"

Pope John Paul II, Rome, 2000

The Message of Fatima

Two of the three shepherd children of Fatima, Saint Francisco and Saint Jacinta, were 9 and 10 years old when they died. That makes them the youngest people ever canonized by the Church, apart from martyrs.

In the year 2000, when Pope John Paul II arrived in Rome to beatify them, he was met by throngs of children who were dressed like Francisco and Jacinta.

Heaven asks children to do big things!

"Dear boys and girls, I see so many of you dressed like Francisco and Jacinta. You look very nice!" he told them. "But you will change your clothes and the little shepherds will disappear. They should not disappear, should they?"

"No!" the children answered.

"Our Lady needs you—all!" he said. Then he told them everything they need to do to change the world.

The story of Fatima is the story how Catholic children dramatically changed history in our times by being obedient to Our Lady of Fatima's plan from Heaven.

Our families can change history again. In your hands you hold the action plan you need. All we must do is ask as Lucia did, every time Our Lady appeared:

"What would you like me to do?"

Our Lady looked to be about 17 years old, always "pleasant, but sad."

From an interview with Lucia

The Story of FATIMA

Our Lady teaches us to pray and sacrifice for sinners.

The Sun, the Crowd and the Children

"The silver sun … was seen to whirl and turn in the circle of broken clouds," reported the newspaper of Lisbon, Portugal. "People wept and prayed with uncovered heads, in the presence of a miracle they had awaited."

The newspaper was reporting on the Miracle of the Sun. It happened on October 13, 1917, in Fatima, Portugal, and was witnessed by tens of thousands of people. Even unbelievers saw it.

One of those witnesses was a professor of natural sciences from a nearby university. He described the miracle this way: "The sun, whirling, seemed to loosen itself from the firmament and advance threateningly upon the earth as if to crush us with its huge fiery weight."

The crowds of people screamed in fright, he said. But then they cheered with joy. They were not crushed by the sun. Instead, their hearts were transformed by one of the most powerful public miracles of all time.

And in the center of that crowd were three little shepherd children: Francisco and Jacinta Marto and their cousin Lucia dos Santos.

Five months earlier, on May 13, 1917, the three children had seen a "Lady dressed in white" hovering over a tree in a field. The Lady returned five more times. During the year before that, they had been visited three times by an angel who had even given them Holy Communion.

Nine visits from Heaven. And each visit brought new messages from God to earth, revealed new prayers, and taught new lessons which can transform our families today

O MILAGRE DE FÁTIMA

Varios aspectos do povo ajoelhado e orando no momento de descobrir o sol e de se dar o fenomeno que tanto impressionou a multidão.

no vagalhão colossal d'aquele povo que ali se juntou a 15 de outubro. O teu racionalismo sofreu um formidavel embate e queres estabelecer uma opinião segura socorrendo-te de depoimentos insuspeitos como o meu, pois que entre li apenas no desempenho de uma missão bem dificil, tal a de relatar imparcialmente para um grande diario, O Seculo, os factos que dante de mim se desenrolassem e tudo quanto de curioso e de eluciclativo a eles se prendesse.

(Carta a aiguem que pede um testemunho insuspeito).

Quebrando um silencio de mais de vinte anos e com a invocação dos longinquos e saudosos tempos em que convivemos n'uma fraternal camaradagem, iluminada então pela fé comum e fortalecida por identicos propositos, escreves-me para que te diga, sincera e minuciosamente, o que vi e ouvi na charneca de Fátima, quando a fama de celestes aparições congregou n'aquele desolado ermo dezenas de milhares de pessoas mais sedentas, segundo creio, de sobrenatural do que impelidas por mera curiosidade ou receosas de um logro... Estão os catolicos em desacordo sobre a importancia e a significação do que presenceraram. Uns convenceram-se de que se tinham cumprido prometimentos do Altar, outros acham-se ainda longe de acreditar ou incontravam-se rafidade de um milagre. Poste um crente na tua juventude e deante de sol-o, Pessoas da familia arrastaram-te a Fátima,

Não ficará por satisfazer a tua desejo, mas decorrido que os mesmos olhos e os mesmos ouvidos não viram nem ouviram coisas diversas, e que raros foram os que ficaram insensiveis á grandeza de semelhante espectação, unico entre nós e de todo o ponto digno de meditação e de estudo...

O que ouvi e me levou a Fátima? Que a Virgem Maria, depois da festa da Ascenção, apareceu a tres crianças que apascentavam gado, duas mocinhas e um rapazete, recomendando-lhes que orassem e prometendo-lhes...

redonder... até os contin...

SPAIN

FATIMA
PORTUGAL

Meet the Shepherd Children of Fatima

Francisco Marto was 9 when the miracle of the sun at Fatima, Portugal, attracted so much attention on October 13, 1917. His little sister, Jacinta, was 7, and their cousin, Lucia dos Santos, was 10.

Much had changed in their lives in the past year and a half. To understand why, and what it has to do with us, we have to go back to Spring 1916.

When the story began, Francisco was 7. He was a good boy, but far from perfect. He liked playing games, but he was never very enthusiastic about them. He liked singing and playing music on a flute and he liked catching lizards and snakes, but he didn't like to pray. Sometimes, he took shortcuts to finish his prayers by saying just the first two words of each prayer in the Rosary.

Jacinta was in some ways the opposite of her brother. She was very enthusiastic, and everybody loved her. But sometimes she would get moody and pout when she didn't get her way. She was very stubborn.

Their cousin Lucia was the older, responsible one. In her own family, she was the youngest of seven children. She had the reputation of being careful to do what she was supposed to do. She loved to sing and even make up her own songs.

The three children were Catholic. They were from Catholic families and lived in a Catholic town. Nobody they knew ever thought about being anything else, so neither did they. The faith was strong where they lived—people knew for certain that Jesus was their Lord and Mary was their mother and that what the Church taught was true.

This was a great blessing in their lives, but they were about to get an even greater blessing—finding out for themselves just how powerful their faith really was.

LUCIA / AGE 10   JACINTA / AGE 7   FRANCISCO / AGE 8

Francisco

Francisco Learns to Pray

It was a cool spring morning in 1916 when Francisco Marto took the sheep out as usual with his little sister and his cousin onto the rocky slopes near the small town of Fatima, Portugal.

He didn't know it then, but he was about to receive a lesson in the three most important virtues: faith, hope and love.

Rain started falling on the children, so they ducked into a cave to keep dry. Francisco probably loved that—a chance to explore. When the rain passed they came out and ate their lunch on a rock. They also prayed, but in a hurry so that they could play.

It was during a game of jacks that a strong wind came, and seemed to bring a white light with it. Francisco was amazed to see an angel appear in that light, an angel that looked like a young man.

"Fear not! I am the Angel of Peace," said the angel. "Pray with me!"

The angel taught them the Pardon Prayer:

> My God, I believe, I adore, I hope and I love You! I ask pardon of You for those who do not believe, do not adore, do not hope and do not love You.

For Francisco, this was especially a lesson in faith. He learned that prayer was not just something you had to do quickly to get back to your real life. God is real, He wants us to talk to Him, and He hears us loud and clear.

"Pray this way," said the Angel. "The Hearts of Jesus and Mary are ready to listen to you."

Pray always and

Francisco Marto
Born: June 12, 1908
Died: April 4, 1919 (age 10)

Beatified: March 13, 2000, by Pope Saint John Paul II
Canonized: May 13, 2017, by Pope Francis
Feast Day: February 20

Faith, Prayer and Angels

Jesus on Prayer

"Whatever you ask in prayer, you will receive, if you have faith."
Matthew 21:22

Act of Faith

My God, I believe in You and all that Your Church teaches, because You
have said it, and Your word is true.

The Church Teaches

We each receive the three theological virtues at baptism: faith, hope and
love. Through faith we freely commit ourselves to God. Those with faith
seek to know and do the will of God because "faith works through love."

The angels are purely spiritual creatures. They are immortal, and usually
invisible, messengers of God.

To adore God means to acknowledge Him as Creator and Savior, the Lord
and Master of everything that exists. Angels continually adore God, and we
often join their prayer, for instance in the Sanctus prayer (the "Holy, Holy,
Holy") at Mass.

Because she is so close to the Father, Son and Holy Spirit, the Church loves
to pray with and through the Virgin Mary.

never lose heart.

Jacinta

Jacinta Learns to Sacrifice

Francisco's sister, Jacinta, was 6 when she saw the angel the first time he visited—and she was still 6 when he visited again.

The people of many nations, such as Portugal, take a regular afternoon rest, called a "siesta," during the hottest time of the day. It was during siesta time on a hot summer day when the angel visited again. The three children were playing by the well near Lucia's house when suddenly the angel—again, like a young man, gleaming white—was at their side.

The children weren't sleeping, but what the angel said was a wake-up call—a spiritual wake-up call.

> What are you doing? You must pray! Pray! The hearts of Jesus and Mary have merciful designs for you. You must offer your prayers and sacrifices to God, the Most High.

This was a message which all of the children, and Jacinta, in particular, would take very much to heart in the months and years that followed.

The angel was teaching the children about hope. God has a plan for each of us, God wants to bring mercy to the world, and by offering sacrifices we cooperate with His plan.

The angel said:

> In every way you can offer sacrifice to God in reparation for the sins by which He is offended, and in supplication for sinners. In this way you will bring peace to our country, for I am its guardian angel, the Angel of Portugal. Above all, bear and accept with patience the sufferings God will send you.

The children started to realize how important they were in God's eyes—and how much their prayers and sacrifices can do for others.

Offer up your sufferings

Jacinta Marto
Born: March 11, 1910
Died February 20, 1920 (age 9)

Beatified: March 13, 2000, by Pope Saint John Paul II
Canonized: May 13, 2017, by Pope Francis
Feast Day: February 20

Hope and Suffering

Jesus on Sacrifice

"If any want to become My followers, let them deny themselves and take up their cross daily and follow Me." Luke 9:23

Act of Hope

My God, I hope in You, for grace and for glory, because of Your promises, Your mercy and Your power.

The Church Teaches

Hope is the theological virtue by which we desire and await from God eternal life as our happiness. Hope means trusting in Christ's promises and relying on the help of the grace of the Holy Spirit to achieve them.

Jesus Christ sacrificed Himself for sinners, so that we would have the hope of Heaven—and He asks us to join in His sacrifice.

Saint Basil the Great said, "Beside each believer stands an angel as a protector and shepherd leading him to life." The Church calls these our Guardian Angels.

To offer reparations to God means to help make up for what is owed to God by the serious sins that people do.

to God, the Most High.

Lucia

Communion from the Angel

The third and final visit of the angel came in early Autumn. The children were already much changed. Now, they prayed with much greater devotion when they took their sheep to graze — and they loved to pray as the angel had taught them.

Lucia, 10, was a leader in this. She was already very spiritually aware, even before the apparitions. She was the only one of the children who had received her First Communion. She never forgot that day. "I felt as though transformed in God," she said. "I only felt at home where I could recall the delights of my first communion."

When the angel came that fall, the children no longer needed a wake-up call. They were kneeling together and praying the Pardon Prayer when a bright light surrounded them.

This time the angel was holding a chalice with a host dripping blood into it.

He taught them "The Angel's Prayer" which you can find in the back of this book.

Then, a remarkable thing happened. The angel gave communion to each of the children, saying:

> "Eat and drink the Body and Blood of Jesus Christ terribly outraged by the ingratitude of men. Offer reparation for their sakes and console God."

Now Francisco and Jacinta had reason to remember their First Communion the way Lucia already did. And when they did, they always remembered the angel's last two words: "Console God."

God was doing what He always does when the Church offers communion to children.

He was preparing them to do something big.

Jesus is truly present

Lucia de Jesus dos Santos
Born: March 28, 1907
Died: February 13, 2005 (age 97)

Entered Carmelite Convent: May 31, 1949
Religious Name: Sister Maria Lucia of Jesus and the Immaculate Heart
Cause for sainthood began: April 30, 2008

Love and the Eucharist

Jesus is Consoled when Sinners Repent

"I tell you, there will be more joy in Heaven over one sinner who repents than over ninety-nine righteous persons who need no repentance." Luke 15:7

Act of Charity

My God, because You are so good, I love You with all my heart, and for Your sake, I love my neighbor as myself.

The Church Teaches

Love (or charity) is the theological virtue by which we love God above all things and our neighbor as ourselves for the love of God.

Jesus knew us and loved us with a human heart. His heart, pierced for our salvation, is the symbol of that infinite love with which He loves the Father and each one of us. His mother joined herself with His sacrifice in her heart.

In the Eucharist, the body, blood, soul and divinity of Christ is really present and shared with the faithful, inviting us to unite our suffering, prayers and work, to Christ's sacrifice.

Receiving communion unites us with Jesus and strengthens our love for God and each other.

in the Most Holy Eucharist

Console Jesus

The Angel's Prayer

Most Holy Trinity, Father, Son and Holy Spirit, I adore You profoundly, and I offer You the Most Precious Body, Blood, Soul and Divinity of Jesus Christ, present in all the tabernacles of the world, in reparation for the outrages, sacrileges and indifference by which He is offended. And by the infinite merits of His Most Sacred Heart and the Immaculate Heart of Mary, I beg the conversion of poor sinners.

"Eat and drink the Body and Blood of Jesus Christ terribly outraged by the ingratitude of men. Offer reparation for their sakes and console God."

Jesus, I adore You!

A Day Filled With Light

It was nearly a year later, on May 13, 1917, when Francisco, Jacinta and Lucia got another Heavenly visitor. It was a bright Sunday with big blue skies, and the children once again hurried through their prayers so they could play.

How quickly we forget! They were praying a "shortcut" Rosary again, using just the names of the prayers.

But at around noon a flash of light made them fear a storm was coming. They started herding their sheep home when another flash came. A beautiful lady—filled with and surrounded by light—appeared over a holm oak tree and said "Fear not! I will not harm you."

Lucia asked her, "Where are you from?" and "What do you want of me?" She answered:

> I come from Heaven. I want you to return here on the thirteenth of the month for the next six months, and at the very same hour. Later I shall tell you who I am, and what it is that I most desire.

Francisco didn't hear Our Lady, but Lucia did—and her own questions came tumbling out. "Will I go to Heaven?" she asked. "Yes, you will," came the answer. "And Jacinta?" "She will go, too." "And Francisco?" "Francisco too, my dear, but he will have many Rosaries to say."

As Our Lady looked lovingly but sadly at Francisco, Lucia thought of two friends who had died. "Is Maria Neves in Heaven?" "Yes, she is." And Amelia? "She is in Purgatory," Our Lady said, then asked:

> Will you offer yourselves to God, and bear all the sufferings He sends you—in atonement for all the sins that offend Him and for the conversion of sinners?

"Oh, we will, we will!" said the children. Our Lady responded:

> Then you will have a great deal to suffer, but the grace of God will be with you and will strengthen you.

Then Our Lady's hands opened and a Heavenly light shown on the children from them. Together they dropped to their knees and prayed together. Then our Lady gave them a final message before departing:

> Say the Rosary every day, to bring peace to the world and an end to the war.

Children Can Change the World

The Miracle

Ever since 1917, devotion to Our Lady of Fatima has grown. Every pope since then has promoted the Fatima message. Her shrine has become one of the most popular pilgrimage sites in Europe.

On May 13, 1981—the anniversary of Our Lady of Fatima's first appearance—a terrorist shot Pope John Paul II in Saint Peter's Square. The Pope was rushed to the hospital.

Doctors said the bullet barely missed his internal organs. The Pope said Our Lady of Fatima had saved his life.

After doctors removed the bullet, the Pope brought it to the statue of Our Lady of Fatima and placed it in her crown.

Pope Benedict and Pope Francis

Pope Francis entrusted his pontificate to Our Lady of Fatima on May 13, 2013.

Pope Benedict said: "A stern warning has been launched from that place [Fatima] that is directed against the prevailing frivolity, a summons to the seriousness of life, of history, to the perils that threaten humanity. It is that which Jesus Himself recalls very frequently: 'Unless you repent, you will all perish.'"

The grace of God will be with you and will strengthen you.

A Saint Anthony's Day Visit

June 13, 1917, one month later, was a Wednesday, two days after Francisco's 9th birthday—but most importantly for the village, it was the feast of Saint Anthony of Padua, who was born in Portugal and was loved and feasted in his native land.

Things had not gone well for the three shepherd children after the first apparition. They agreed not to tell what had happened, but Jacinta could not help herself. She told her parents everything, and soon the whole town knew.

Rather than being overjoyed at the news, most people were highly skeptical. Many of them thought the children were making it up. Lucia suffered the moSaint Her mother was very angry at her for speaking about Heavenly visions, and she took her to the local parish priest, Father Ferreira. He was also skeptical and even thought the vision might be from the Devil, but he refused to rule out the children's story. The Church is very cautious but open to God's works.

Francisco and Jacinta's father, Ti Marto, however, believed the children right away. He is now called the first disciple of Fatima.

At any rate, everyone thought the children would get caught up in the Saint Anthony festival and forget about the apparition. But they did not forget. They left the fun to head back to the Cova de Iria where they first saw Our Lady.

Soon, they saw her again. Lucia asked, "Please tell me, Madam, what it is that you want of me?" Our Lady repeated that they should come on the 13th of each month and to say the Rosary every day. Then she taught them a new prayer for the Rosary:

> And after each one of the mysteries, my children, I want you to pray in this way: 'O my Jesus, forgive us. Save us from the fire of Hell. Take all souls to Heaven, especially those who are most in need.'

Then, she told Lucia, "I want you to learn to read and write, and later I will tell you what else I want of you."

Lucia asked, "Will you take us to Heaven?" "Yes, I shall take Jacinta and Francisco soon, but you will remain a little longer, since Jesus wishes you to make me known and loved on earth. He wishes also for you to establish devotion in the world to my Immaculate Heart."

Lucia was sad. She asked, "Must I remain in the world alone?"

Not alone, my child, and you must not be sad. I will be with you always, and my Immaculate Heart will be your comfort and the way which will lead you to God.

Again, she shared the beautiful light that filled them with peace.

Children Can Change the World

Our Lady's Protection

The story of Fatima is the story of a concerned mother eager to warn her children of danger and tell them everything will be all right.

The prayer Our Lady of Fatima taught was taken up by Catholics everywhere. Many began to say the Rosary every day, with the added prayer after each decade.

Pope John Paul II visited the terrorist who shot him in the man's prison cell, and forgave him.

"Why didn't you die?" asked the terroriSaint "One hand fired the shot, another guided it," said the Pope.

Pray the Rosary Every Day

"This daily 'pause for prayer' with the family ... is a spiritual aid which should not be underestimated. I look to all of you, brothers and sisters of every state of life, to you, Christian families, to you, the sick and elderly, and to you, young people: confidently take up the Rosary once again. May this appeal of mine not go unheard!" Saint John Paul II, *Letter on the Rosary*

I will be with you always ...

Visions and Secrets

By the time of the July 13, 1917, apparition, thousands came to pray with the children in the Cova. Many others did not believe. The parish pastor remained skeptical.

When Our Lady appeared, Lucia asked for a miracle "so that everyone will know for certain that you have appeared to us." Our Lady said:

> You must come here every month, and in October I will tell you who I am and what I want. I will then perform a miracle so that all may believe.

Then, Our Lady opened her hands again, and revealed three visions to the children, asking them to keep them secret.

Lucia described the first secret this way: "The rays of light seemed to penetrate the earth, and we saw as it were a sea of fire. Plunged in this fire were demons and souls in human form." It lasted a moment, then Our Lady said:

> You have seen Hell, where the souls of poor sinners go. It is to save them that God wants to establish in the world devotion to my Immaculate Heart. If you do what I tell you, many souls will be saved, and there will be peace.

In the second secret, she asked for the consecration of Russia and warned about World War II:

> This war will end, but if men do not refrain from offending God, another and more terrible war will begin ...

The third secret was only revealed by Lucia many years later. In it, the children saw "an Angel with a flaming sword in his left hand" who cried out "Penance, Penance, Penance!" Then, they saw a "bishop in white"— the Pope—walking past martyrs "with halting step, afflicted with pain and sorrow." He knelt and prayed at a giant cross. Then the pope himself was shot.

The three secrets helped many believe in Fatima. People said, "How could these children invent such visions? How could they know so much about world affairs?"

Yet every vision they had has proven true.

Children Can Change the World

Vision and Predictions

Our Lady warned the children about some terrible truths.

Hell. Our Lady was right to warn of Hell. Jesus often spoke of Hell, which exists because God made us truly free to accept or reject His happiness. God gave us everything—who we are and what we have—to be happy with Him. Jesus compared us to tenants who a landlord left in charge of a vineyard. What if we took everything he gave us and used it to attack him? This is what we do when we sin.

War. World WarI was raging during the time of the Fatima apparitions, but Our Lady predicted that World War II would soon follow, as well as the spread of Russia's atheistic Soviet communism, which made many nations disappear. She said World War II would begin after "a night that is lit by a strange and unknown light." Fighting began after a remarkably bright aurora borealis (described as "a curtain of fire") in January of 1938.

Martyrs. In addition to the assassination attempt on the pope, Our Lady predicted a new time of martyrs. Starting with the 20th century, our times have seen more Christian martyrs than the rest of history put together.

Conversion and Repentance

"The message of Fatima is a call to conversion and repentance, as in the Gospel."
—Pope John Paul II

Visions and Secrets are meant to help people believe the truth.

Trouble and a Delay

The August 1917 apparition of Our Lady was delayed by a great upheaval in the lives of Francisco, Jacinta and Lucia. Many people were asking for prayers, and many people were leaving money at the Cova.

In July, Lucia had asked if a crippled boy would be healed. Our Lady had said: "No. Neither of his infirmity nor of his poverty will he be cured, and he must be certain to say the Rosary with his family every day." She had also asked about a sick woman who wanted to be taken to Heaven. Our Lady had said: "Tell her not to be in a hurry. Tell her I know very well when I shall come to fetch her."

Then, there were dark trials for the children. On August 13, a local official tricked them, saying he would drive them to the Cova. Instead, he took them to his office and threatened to kill them if they didn't reveal their secrets. He badgered them with questions for days and even locked them in jail.

The children were very brave. They were ready to die for their faith. They even said the Rosary with prisoners. All the same, they were not at the Cova on August 13, so they did not see Our Lady.

On August 19, 1917, Lucia, Francisco, and his brother John took the sheep out to Valinhos, near the place they saw the angel. Suddenly, Our Lady appeared. Lucia sent John to go get Jacinta. Our Lady said:

> Come again to the Cova da Iria on the thirteenth of next month, my child, and continue to say the Rosary every day. In the last month I will perform a miracle so that all may believe.

Lucia asked again about cures and mentioned the money at the Cova. "Some I will cure this year," said Our Lady, and said to use the money for specific celebrations of Our Lady of the Rosary on October 7 and to help build a chapel. Then, her expression turned sad. Our Lady said:

> Pray, pray very much, and make sacrifices for sinners; for many souls go to hell, because there are none to sacrifice themselves and to pray for them.

Children Can Change the World

Faith in Practice

Many miraculous cures have been documented as the result of prayers. The Church says it is our duty to ask God to help others, as Mary did—and particularly to pray for the sick.

At the same time, God is not like a genie who grants all of our wishes. He is our infinitely wise Father.

Jesus says, "Everyone who asks, receives," then adds that God will only give us what is truly good for us, saying "Which one of you would hand his son a stone when he asks for a loaf of bread, or a snake when he asks for a fish?" (Matthew 7:8-10)

"Do not be troubled if you do not immediately receive from God what you ask Him," says the Catechism. "He desires to do something even greater for you, while you cling to Him in prayer."

Prayer and Sacrifice

"Prayer joined to sacrifice constitutes the most powerful force in human history." —Pope Saint John Paul II

Pray, pray very much.
Make sacrifices for sinners.

Pushing Through the Crowds

By September 13, 1917, word had spread far and wide about the Fatima apparitions. It was impossible for the three children to simply come to the Cova and pray. They had to push through a crowd of 25,000, many of the people begging the children to bring their petitions to Our Lady.

It was only with the help of men who made an opening for them through the crowds that the three children made it to the spot for the apparition at all.

They began to lead the people in a Rosary when the flash of light came, and then Mary appeared on the holm oak tree.

"What do you want of me?" asked Lucia as she always did. Our Lady answered:

> Continue the Rosary, my children. Say it every day that the war may end. In October Our Lord will come, as well as Our Lady of Sorrows and Our Lady of Mount Carmel. Saint Joseph will appear with the Child Jesus to bless the world.

The children loved seeing the angel, but even more seeing Mary. They could now look forward to seeing Mary in each of these manifestations of her life: Our Lady of Sorrows, when she joined the suffering of her son in her life with Him and at the Cross, and Our Lady of Mount Carmel, when she gave the world the scapular, a small woolen devotional worn around the neck like a necklace.

They also would get to see Saint Joseph, Patron of the Church. But, to see Jesus would be the best of all!

Last, Our Lady gave the children some advice. They had begun to wear cords around their waists. It caused them extra suffering which they could offer up to Our Lord. However, they had also started wearing the cords at night. Our Lady said:

> God is pleased with your sacrifices, but He does not want you to wear the cords to bed. Keep them on during the day.

Lucia again brought petitions to Our Lady's attention. She answered:

> Some I will cure, and some I will not. In October I will perform a miracle so that all may believe.

This time, as Our Lady retreated from them, Lucia pointed the crowd to where her figure was disappearing and said, "If you want to see Our Lady, look!"

Children Can Change the World

Penance

True freedom is the ability to become what God wants us to be, and true happiness is found in the will of God.

But we fool ourselves into thinking that freedom means doing whatever we want. This just makes us a slave to whatever we want. We also fool ourselves into thinking earthly pleasures will make us happy. But this always leave us sad.

This is why we do penance and mortify ourselves. Only by offering up sacrifices do we gain the ability to free ourselves to embrace real happiness.

Many saints, including Saint John Paul II, have taken on special mortifications. But like Saint Francisco and Saint Jacinta, they always ask a wise guide (like parents or their parish priest) if this is good for them, and never do more than is recommended for them.

Pope Benedict on Fatima and Penance

"In a conversation with me Sister Lucia said that it appeared ever more clearly to her that the purpose of all the apparitions was to help people to grow more and more in faith, hope and love—everything else was intended to lead to this." Cardinal Joseph Ratzinger (Pope Benedict XVI), *Message of Fatima*

True happiness is found in doing what God wants you to do.

The Miracle of the Sun

In a way, the October 13, 1917, apparition summed up all the others.

The apparitions had always been a hardship. Today was the hardest ever. Rain had poured down starting the day before, meaning the children had to trudge through mud.

The crowds were overwhelming: 70,000 people came to the Cova, including many skeptics who wanted to be the first to ridicule the children when the miracle failed to appear.

Lucia's mother also still did not believe. She brought Lucia to Confession the day before. She feared the crowds would kill her daughter in their outrage at being fooled.

Then, in the early afternoon, Our Lady of Fatima appeared once again. "What do you want of me?" asked Lucia. Our Lady answered:

> I want a chapel built here in my honor. I want you to continue saying the Rosary every day. The war will end soon, and the soldiers will return to their homes.

"Will you tell me your name?" asked Lucia. She answered: "I am the Lady of the Rosary."

Lucia said, "I have many petitions from many people. Will you grant them?" Our Lady answered:

> Some I shall grant, and others I must deny. People must amend their lives and ask pardon for their sins. They must not offend Our Lord any more, for He is already too much offended!

"And is that all you have to ask?" Lucia asked. Our Lady said, "There is nothing more."

Our Lady rose to the East and turned her palms to the sky. Suddenly, the sun burst through the clouds. "Look at the sun!" shouted Lucia.

The children saw Our Lady of Fatima depart, and then Saint Joseph and the Child Jesus appeared. Our Lady also appeared beside the sun, wearing blue. Saint Joseph and the Child Jesus made the Sign of the Cross, blessing the world. Then, Our Lady of Sorrows appeared. Finally, only Lucia saw Our Lady of Mount Carmel.

The crowd saw none of that: Instead, they saw the sun pulsate, spin and fill the world with color. Then, they saw it plummet to the ground. The crowd's fear turned to delight as they found that the ground, miraculously, was no longer muddy.

Like before, the hardship of the apparitions had turned to joy. One other thing remained constant: Francisco and Jacinta's father Ti, the first to believe the children, was there, believing still.

"The sun painted the world in different colors," he described it later. "It moved and danced in the sky!"

Children Can Change the World

A Message of Hope

The miracle convinced many people, worldwide, to repent, believe in the Catholic faith, and say the Rosary daily for peace.

A chapel was built at the site of the apparitions, and opened three years later. Today, it is an enormous basilica and one of the world's most popular Catholic shrines.

Several popes have consecrated the world and Russia to the Immaculate Heart, as Our Lady of Fatima requested: Pope Pius XII (1942), Pope John Paul II (1984), Pope Benedict XVI (2010) and Pope Francis (2013) consecrated the world to the Immaculate Heart, with Pius XII also specifically consecrating "the peoples of Russia" in 1952.

The October 1917 blessing of the world reminds us that the message of Fatima is a message of hope. As she said earlier: "In the end my Immaculate Heart will triumph. The Holy Father will consecrate Russia to me, and she will be converted, and the world will enjoy a period of peace."

Never Forget Fatima

At Fatima, "Mary's appeal is not for just once. Her appeal must be taken up by generation after generation, in accordance with the ever new 'signs of the times.' It must be unceasingly returned to. It must ever be taken up anew." —Saint John Paul II

Pray the Rosary

The Fatima Prayer

Oh My Jesus, forgive us, save us from the fire of Hell. Lead all souls to Heaven, especially those who are most in need.

"Pray, pray very much, and make sacrifices for sinners; for many souls go to hell, because there are none to sacrifice themselves and to pray for them."

—Our Lady of Fatima

Jesus, I am sorry for my sins!

Saint Francisco: The Rest of the Story

The Brother

Francisco died when he was 10, on April 4, 1919. Pope Francis canonized him on May 13, 2017, so we can now call him "Saint Francisco Marto."

The last years of his life were profoundly affected by the Fatima apparitions. He and Jacinta sacrificed very much for sinners, including giving their food away to beggars and enduring physical pain.

Lucia described Francisco as the most contemplative of the three. He was at his happiest when he was with Jesus in the Blessed Sacrament. He especially liked to pray very close to the tabernacle such that he was hidden by the altar. One day when he was walking to school, he seemed sick and unstable. He told Lucia and Jacinta, "You go on. I am going to church to keep company with the hidden Jesus." (Francisco knew that he would not live for much longer, so it was not important for him to go to school.)

"Little Francisco had a great desire to atone for the offences of sinners by striving to be good and by offering his sacrifices and prayers," Saint John Paul II said. "Francisco was motivated by one desire," he added: "to console Jesus and make Him happy."

When he was very sick, Saint Francisco would get out of his bed and pray kneeling on the floor as the angel had taught him. Finally, near the end of his life, he said, "Mamma, I can no longer say the Rosary. I feel like my head is among the clouds."

He received Holy Communion on April 2. Two days later, he said, "Look mamma, look, a light so beautiful, there near the door." Francisco died soon after, with his face lit up with a supernatural light.

Saint John Paul II later said: "Francisco bore without complaining the great sufferings caused by the illness from which he died. It all seemed to him so little to console Jesus: he died with a smile on his lips."

The Words of Saint Francisco Marto

On the apparitions "I loved seeing the Angel, but I love seeing Our Lady even more. What I loved most of all was to see Our Lord in that light from Our Lady which penetrated our hearts. I love God so much! But He is very sad because of so many sins. We must not commit any sins."

On the Heavenly light "We were burning in that light which is God and we were not consumed. What is God like? It is impossible to say. In fact we will never be able to tell people."

On receiving Holy Communion from the Angel "I knew God was in me, but did not know how He was."

When his father asked him one night why he was crying "I was thinking of Jesus who is so sad because of the sins that are committed against Him."

He seemed joyful and content, even when he was sick, so Lucia asked him if he was suffering "Quite a lot, but never mind. I am suffering to console our Lord, and soon I am going to Heaven."

To Jacinta, at the end of his life "I would like to console the Lord and then convert sinners so they will no longer offend the Lord. Soon I will be in Heaven, and when I get there I will console very much Our Lord and Our Lady. You are going to stay here because Our Lady wishes it. Listen. Do everything she tells you."

Saint Jacinta: The Rest of the Story

The Little Sister

Jacinta Marto died on February 20, 1920, when she was 9. She is the youngest non-martyr ever canonized. (Her brother, Saint Francisco, is the next youngest.) Jacinta was filled with a spirit of sacrifice, love for the Heart of Mary, and for the Holy Father and sinners.

Following the Miracle of the Sun, Jacinta made it her personal mission to accept the many requests for prayers pressed upon her.

Saint John Paul said of the many sacrifices she made, "Jacinta had been so deeply moved by the vision of Hell during the apparition of July 13 that no mortification or penance seemed too great to save sinners."

Our Lady appeared to Jacinta four times at home during her months of illness. Our Lady warned Jacinta that she would go to a hospital—not to be cured, she said, but to sacrifice for sinners.

After two months in the hospital, Jacinta returned home, only to develop tuberculosis and get sent to Lisbon to a sick room in an orphanage. To her great joy, she could attend Mass there and see the tabernacle she loved. But then she was transferred to a secular hospital where she died alone; her final sacrifice for sinners.

A nurse who saw her after she died said, "She did not look the same child; she had become radiant and beautiful."

Her body was exhumed twice, the second time 31 years after her death. She was found to be incorrupt—her body had not decayed.

The Words of Saint Jacinta Marto

On Confession "Confession is a sacrament of mercy, and we must confess with joy and truSaint There can be no salvation without Confession."

To her mother, after seeing the vision of Hell "Mother, fly from riches and luxury."

Her frequent advice "Love poverty, and silence."

On the vision of Hell "It is necessary to pray much to save souls from Hell! … How sorry I am for sinners! If I could only show them Hell!"

On sins of the flesh "The sins which cause most souls to go to Hell are the sins of the flesh."

On purity and integrity "To be pure in body means to be chaste, and to be pure in mind means not to commit sins; not to look at what one should not see, not to steal or lie, and always to speak the truth, even if it is hard."

Saint Jacinta called priests to great purity "The Mother of God wants more virgin souls bound by a vow of chastity."

On saving the world "Penance is necessary. If people amend their lives, our Lord will even yet save the world, but if not, punishment will come."

On suffering "Mortification and sacrifice please our Lord very much."

On converting sinners "Oh, how much I love to suffer for love of Our Lord and Our Lady. They greatly love those who suffer for the conversion of sinners."

Sister Lucia: The Rest of the Story

The Cousin

Our Lady of Fatima had predicted that while Francisco and Jacinta would die young, Lucia would lead a long life, and that is just what happened. Lucia died on February 13, 2005, at age 97.

This means that Lucia was the only one of the visionaries to see the predictions of Our Lady come true, including the Second World War and the assassination attempt on the pope.

When she was 14, Lucia and her family moved away from Fatima and she became a boarding student in the school of the Sisters of Saint Dorothy in Vilar. It was during her time with the Sisters of Saint Dorothy that she was again visited by Our Lady and learned about the Five First Saturdays Devotion found later in this booklet.

In 1948, Lucia returned to Fatima quietly, without revealing who she was. She then became a Carmelite sister in Coimbra, Portugal, in 1949, taking the name Sister Maria Lucia of Jesus and the Immaculate Heart.

Our Lady of Fatima had asked Lucia to learn to write in order to spread devotion to the Immaculate Heart of Mary, and Sister Lucia spent her lifetime complying with that requeSaint

When she died, Saint John Paul II and the cardinal who would become Pope Benedict XVI both said that she would go to Heaven. Portugal declared a national day of mourning for the sister.

The Words of Sister Lucia dos Santos

The process toward Sister Lucia's beatification and canonization began soon after her death in 2005.

On the Rosary in our times "The Most Holy Virgin in these last times in which we live has given a new efficacy to the recitation of the Rosary. …There is no problem, I tell you, no matter how difficult it is, that we cannot resolve by the prayer of the Holy Rosary."

On words of love "What is missing in the people who think the Rosary monotonous is love. Anything we do without love is worthless."

Everyday martyrdom "Putting up with any sacrifices that are asked of us in our day-to-day lives becomes a slow martyrdom which purifies us and raises us up to the level of the supernatural. ... We have here an incomparable spiritual richness!"

On Hell "Hell is a reality. It is a supernatural fire and not physical. ... Continue preaching about Hell because Our Lord Himself spoke about Hell, and it is in Sacred Scripture. God does not condemn anyone to Hell. God gave men the liberty to choose, and God respects this human liberty."

On hope "Do not be afraid, because anyone who works for the sanctity of marriage and the family will always be fought and opposed in every way, because this is the decisive issue. However, Our Lady has already crushed Satan's head."

Convert Sinners

The Sacrifice Prayer

Oh my Jesus, I offer this for love of Thee, for the conversion of sinners, and in reparation for the sins committed against the Immaculate Heart of Mary.

Our Lady of Fatima calls all of us to seek the conversion of sinners and the return of souls to God. We can all imitate the beautiful way in which Lucia, Jacinta, and Francisco prayed and sacrificed for sinners.

Pray also for the souls in Purgatory.

Console Jesus.
Convert Sinners.
Commit Myself
to Our Lady.

YOUR FATIMA FAMILY ACTION PLAN
CONSOLE · CONVERT · COMMIT

Console Jesus

At Fatima in the year 2000, Saint John Paul II told the families of the world that they should do three things to imitate the shepherd children of Fatima: console Jesus, convert sinners and commit themselves to Our Lady.

We can console Jesus—just as we can offend Him or make Him sad. We offend and sadden Him when we sin. We console Him when we repent of our sins. Jesus Himself has told us how much joy there is in Heaven when a sinner repents (Luke 15:7).

Jesus asked the Apostles to console Him by staying awake with Him during His Agony in the Garden, but they disappointed Him (Mark 14:32-42).

Jesus asks each of us to spend some time with Him, too—and, thanks to the Eucharist, we can. The *Catechism of the Catholic Church* (No. 1377) reminds us that, "Christ is present whole and entire" in the Blessed Sacrament in the tabernacle. We can console Jesus by visiting Him in the tabernacle.

At Fatima, the angel showed the children a host dripping blood into a chalice (see Luke 22:42-44) and told them to "comfort your God."

Saint Francisco, Saint Jacinta and Lucia did just that, by spending time with "the hidden Jesus" in the Blessed Sacrament.

"Our Lady needs you all to console Jesus, Who is sad because of the bad things done to Him."

Saint John Paul II to families

Visit Jesus in the Blessed Sacrament

Today, families can console Jesus in the way He asked in Gethsemane and in the same way the shepherd children of Fatima did. Children and parents can visit a church with a tabernacle. They can kneel before Jesus in the Blessed Sacrament and pray together.

One idea would be to pray through ACTS silently or out loud:
(Use the examples below or your own words.)

A-C-T-S

A stands for Adoration. *Pray:* Jesus, we adore You, just like the Fatima saints, just like the shepherds and magi at the manger; just like Saint John, Saint Mary Magdalen and your mother at the foot of the Cross.

C stands for Contrition. *Pray:* Jesus, we are so sorry for all of our sins and ask Your mercy on us and on the whole world. In our imagination, we kiss each of Your wounds, saying, "Jesus, I love You. I am so sorry for my sins and the sins of the world." We pray for the conversion of sinners.

T stands for Thanksgiving. *Pray:* Jesus, thank you for our food, shelter, clothing, and most of all for our family and our faith. Please bless those who lack food, shelter, clothing, family or faith. (Then thank Jesus for other blessings you can think of.)

S stands for Supplication, which means asking God for help (also often called petition). *Pray:* Jesus, please bless [names of family members]. Please help increase our faith, hope and love. Please bless all those who most need your help right now.

The Eucharist

THE CHILDREN'S SPONTANEOUS EUCHARISTIC PRAYER

Most Holy Trinity, I adore Thee! My God, my God,
I love Thee in the Most Blessed Sacrament.

MY FATIMA ACTION PLAN
Console Jesus

I will console Jesus by doing the following:

_____

_____

_____

_____

_____

_____

_____

_____

_____

_____

_____

_____

_____

_____

_____

_____

_____

_____

_____

_____

_____

Convert Sinners

In addition to consoling Jesus, Saint John Paul II said all children can imitate Francisco, Jacinta and Lucia by converting sinners. He said:

> "Jesus needs your prayers and your sacrifices for sinners."

Jesus called all of us to work for the conversion of sinners.

"I came not to call the righteous, but sinners to repentance," He said (Luke 5:32). The Catechism (No. 5545) teaches: "He invites [sinners] to that conversion without which one cannot enter the Kingdom."

It is good to think of Fatima and the Divine Mercy devotion of Saint Faustina together. The Fatima children remind us that Hell is a terrible lake of fire where sinners go. Faustina reminds us that God is a beautiful ocean of mercy for sinners who repent.

Sacrifice for Sinners

Christians can unite their sufferings to Christ's sacrifice on the Cross; these sufferings can help atone for our sins and the sins of others through the merits of Christ's Passion. The children of Fatima offered up many sacrifices for the conversion of sinners. We can do this, too. In addition to offering up the difficulties and annoyances of every day, try listing additional actions you can do, then choose to do a few of them each day.

Here are some ideas to get you started:

1. Do an extra chore.

2. Put money in the poor box at church.

3. Skip your dessert or treat or share it with others.

4. Pray frequently for the souls in Purgatory and the conversion of sinners.

5. Smile to cheer people up, even when you don't feel like it, just like Francisco.

6. Don't join others who look at or do something wrong. Suggest something else, then just walk away.

Think up some additional ideas of your own.

Indulgences Help Sinners in the Afterlife

The Church, which has "the power to bind and loose" (see Matthew 16:19) gives us the ability to have an eternal effect on sinners. A plenary indulgence is "a remission before God of the temporal punishment due to sins whose guilt has already been forgiven." A Catholic can obtain an indulgence for himself or for one of the poor souls in Purgatory.

Pious acts for which the Church grants a plenary indulgence:

1. Reading of Scripture for at least one-half hour.

2. Adoration of the Blessed Sacrament for at least one-half hour.

3. Praying for the dead at a cemetery during the first eight days of November.

4. Praying five decades of the Rosary in a church or as a family.

5. Praying the Stations of the Cross in a church.

To receive an indulgence for these acts, a Catholic must:

1. Be in the state of grace

2. Have the interior disposition of complete detachment from sin, even venial sin

3. Go to Confession

4. Receive Holy Communion

5. Pray for the intentions of the Pope (any prayer may be chosen)

It is appropriate, but not necessary, that the sacramental Confession and especially Holy Communion and the prayer for the Pope's intentions take place on the same day that the indulgenced work is performed; but it is sufficient that these sacred rites and prayers be carried out within several days (about 20) before or after the indulgenced act.

One sacramental Confession suffices for several plenary indulgences, but a separate Holy Communion and a separate prayer for the Holy Father's intentions are required for each plenary indulgence.

MY FATIMA ACTION PLAN
Convert Sinners

I will convert sinners by doing the following:

_____

_____

_____

_____

_____

_____

_____

_____

_____

_____

_____

_____

_____

_____

_____

_____

_____

Committing to Mary

In addition to consoling Jesus and converting sinners, Saint John Paul II said to imitate Francisco, Jacinta, and Lucia by committing our time to Jesus through Mary. He said:

> "Ask your parents and teachers to enroll you in the 'school' of Our Lady, so that she can teach you to be like the little shepherds, who tried to do whatever she asked them. I tell you that 'one makes more progress in a short time of submission and dependence on Mary than during entire years of personal initiatives, relying on oneself alone' (Saint Louis de Montfort, *True Devotion*). This was how the little shepherds became saints so quickly."

Jacinta said the same thing more simply: "I so love the Immaculate Heart of Mary, the heart of our Mother in Heaven! … If I could only put it into the hearts of all!"

Pray the Rosary Every Day

Pope Saint John Paul II said the rosary "has all the depth of the Gospel message in its entirety." Through it we are "remembering Christ with Mary" and "learning Christ from Mary" as each individual mystery directs our "imagination … towards a particular episode or moment in the life of Christ."

The Rosary teaches us to imitate Mary's "Yes" to God in *The Annunciation,* her love of neighbor in *The Visitation,* and her sacrificial heart in *The Nativity.* *The Presentation in the Temple* teaches us to imitate her devotion to God and *The Finding in the Temple* teaches us to imitate Jesus's commitment to His mother (see Luke 2:52).

When Jesus begins His public ministry at *The Wedding Feast at Cana,* Mary says, "Do whatever He tells you" (John 2:5). When He ends His public ministry with *The Resurrection* and *The Ascension*, Mary prays with the Apostles for the Holy Spirit, then leads the way to Heaven in *The Assumption* and *The Coronation.*

Both Saint Teresa of Calcutta and Saint John Paul II repeated this advice often: "The family that prays together, stays together." The daily family Rosary gathers us together in quiet, focused attention as we give ourselves to God in the Our Father and commit ourselves to Our Lady in the Hail Mary.

Complete the Five First Saturdays

Our Lady appeared with the Child Jesus to Lucia at her first convent in Pontevedra, Spain, on Dec. 10, 1925. The Child Jesus said: "Have compassion on the heart of your most holy mother, covered with thorns with which ungrateful men pierce it at every moment, and there is no one to make an act of reparation."

Our Lady then told Sister Lucia she would "assist at the hour of death with the graces necessary for salvation" all those who complete the Five First Saturdays.

To complete this devotion, there are **four things** you must do, and they are to be done on the **First Saturdays of five months in a row**.

1. **Go to Confession**
2. **Receive Holy Communion**
3. **Pray 5 Decades of the Rosary**
4. **"Keep our Blessed Mother company" for 15 minutes** by meditating on the mysteries of the Rosary with the intention of offering reparation to her. *This is a separate prayer time from praying the rosary, though.*

The Morning Offering

Offering yourself each day to Jesus through the Immaculate Heart of Mary is a beautiful daily commitment.

Oh, my Jesus, through the Immaculate Heart of Mary,
I offer You my prayers, works, joys, and sufferings of this day.
In union with the Holy Sacrifice of the Mass throughout the world,
I offer them for all the intentions of Your Sacred Heart,
for the intentions of my family and friends, and for the intentions
of our Holy Father, the Pope. Amen.

MY FATIMA ACTION PLAN

Commit to Mary

I will commit myself and my time to the
Blessed Virgin Mary by doing the following:

_____

_____

_____

_____

_____

_____

_____

_____

_____

_____

_____

_____

_____

_____

_____

The Story Continues ...

A Concerned Mother

Jesus said from the Cross, "Behold, your mother!" (John 19:27)

The story of Fatima is the story of a concerned mother eager to protect her children and tell them that everything will be all right.

"You will have to suffer a lot, but the grace of God will be your comfort," Our Lady of Fatima said to the children. She also told Lucia: "Don't be discouraged, I will not abandon you ever. My Immaculate Heart will be your refuge."

She also revealed how the story will end: "In the end, my Immaculate Heart will triumph ... and a time of peace will be granted to the world."

That is good news. Our mother wants us to be safe—and she says everything will be alright.

Be Encouraged ...

Jesus said, "Fear not, little flock, for it is your Father's good pleasure to give you the Kingdom." (Luke 12:32)

Jesus Christ, the Son of God, came to earth to save sinners—and to invite you and your family to help. Again and again, He said: "Do not be afraid!"

The times we live in have been called "the time of great mercy," because, as Saint Paul put it: "Where sin increases, grace abounds all the more." (Romans 5:20)

Evil never wins. With Jesus Christ on our side, there is no reason to fear.

A Secret Mission ...

Jesus prayed, "Father ... to You I offer praise; for what You have hidden from the learned and the clever You have revealed to the merest children." (Mt 11: 25)

Why did Our Lady of Fatima reveal the secrets of Heaven to three ordinary shepherd children? The reason is clear. Jesus, Mary and Saint Joseph see children as supremely important—and they have a special mission for them.

The great men and women of the world have always concocted their plans, but children have always quietly carried the day—from the Baby Jesus in the manger to the shepherd children of Fatima, from the martyred children of Rome to today's new Franciscos and Jacintas.

A Call to Faith ...

Jesus told us, "All things are possible to him who believes." (Mark 9:23)

Alone we can do nothing. With God, nothing is impossible. He sent messengers from Heaven entrusting three small children with so much: New prayers. New devotions. A vision of eternity to inspire millions. A mission to change the world.

This mission was confirmed with amazing signs and wonders that caught the whole world's attention, to increase our faith in the great love and beautiful destiny God has planned for His world.

Take up the offer of Our Lady of Fatima. Console Jesus, convert sinners, and embrace your Mother. She wants what is best for you.

The Story Continues ... with You!

A Light From Heaven to Follow and Share

Not long ago, an angel was sent three times to visit shepherd children in a small town in Portugal, to prepare the way for a "Woman clothed with the sun" (Revelation 12) who would follow. The oldest child, Lucia, said Our Lady was "all light," filled with different colors of light—even "flesh-colored light." Her clothing was "a reflection of the light within." Light came from her hands to illuminate the deepest mysteries of God, and the children were changed, utterly.

But those nine visits from Heaven were not just for them. They were sent on a mission to transform families ... a mission to transform the world. Heaven is inviting each and every one of us to join in that mission—if only we will listen.

Dear Lucia, Jacinta, and Francisco,
help us to love Jesus as you do!

"Our Lord and Our Lady ... greatly love those who suffer for the conversion of sinners."

Jacinta on Suffering

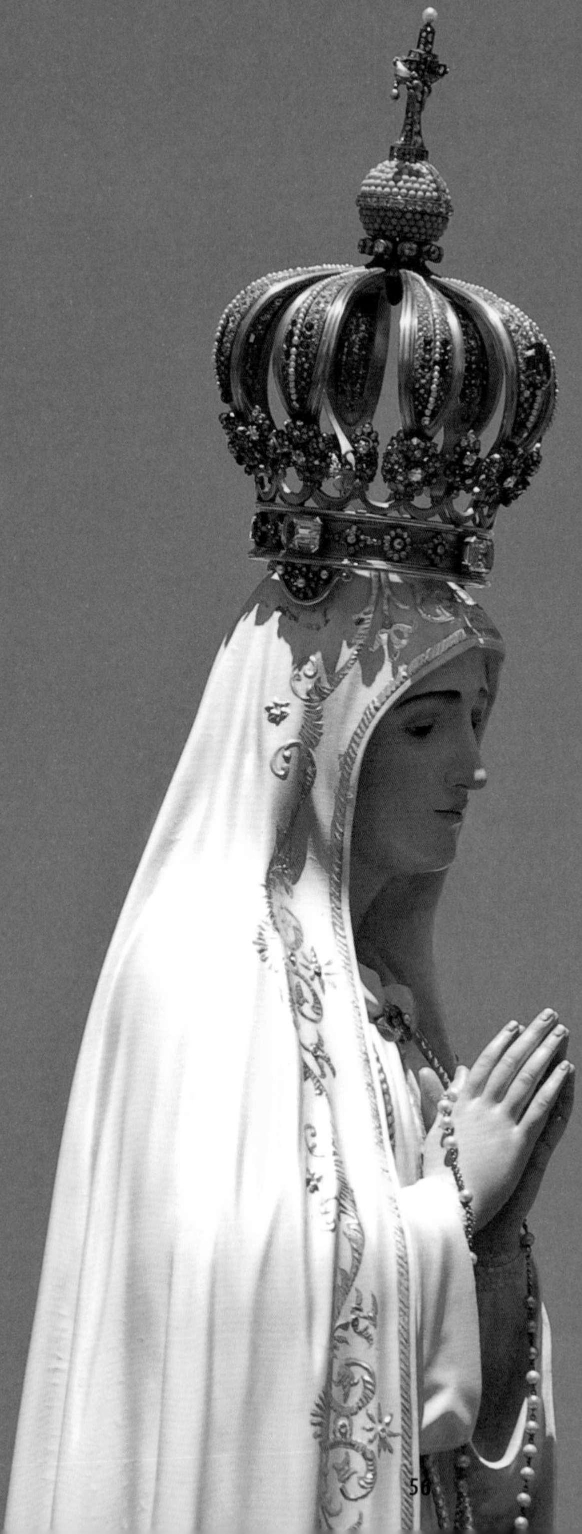

THE FATIMA PRAYERS

THE PARDON PRAYER

My God, I believe, I adore, I hope and I love Thee! I ask pardon for those who do not believe, do not adore, do not hope and do not love Thee.

THE ANGEL'S PRAYER

Most Holy Trinity, Father, Son and Holy Spirit, I adore Thee profoundly. I offer Thee the most precious Body, Blood, Soul and Divinity of Jesus Christ, present in all the tabernacles of the world, in reparation for the outrages, sacrileges, and indifference whereby He is offended. And through the infinite merits of His Most Sacred Heart and the Immaculate Heart of Mary, I beg of Thee the conversion of poor sinners.

THE CHILDREN'S SPONTANEOUS EUCHARISTIC PRAYER

Most Holy Trinity, I adore Thee! My God, my God, I love Thee in the Most Blessed Sacrament.

THE SACRIFICE PRAYER

Oh my Jesus, I offer this for love of Thee, for the conversion of sinners, and in reparation for the sins committed against the Immaculate Heart of Mary.

THE DECADE PRAYER

Oh My Jesus, forgive us, save us from the fire of Hell. Lead all souls to Heaven, especially those who are most in need.

Resources and Further Reading

The story of Fatima and the quotes from the three visionaries and others came primarily from the following sources, which are highly recommended for digging deeper into the details of the apparitions and personalities of Saint Francisco Marto, Saint Jacinta Marto, and Lucia dos Santos.

O'Boyle, Donna-Marie Cooper.
Our Lady's Message to Three Shepherd Children and the World.
Sophia Institute, 2017.

Apostoli, Andrew.
Fatima for Today:
The Urgent Marian Message of Hope.
Ignatius, 2010.

McGlynn, Thomas.
Vision of Fatima.
Sophia Institute, 2017.

Górny, Grzegorz.
Fatima Mysteries:
Mary's Message to the Modern Age.
Ignatius; Rosikon, 2017.

Cirrincione, Joseph, and Thomas Nelson.
Saint Joseph, Fatima and Fatherhood:
Reflections on the Miracle of the Sun.
TAN, 1989.

Cirrincione, Joseph.
Blessed Francisco Marto of Fatima.
TAN, 1994.

Cirrincione, Joseph.
Blessed Jacinta Marto of Fatima.
TAN, 1992.

Santos, Lucia.
Fatima in Lucia's Own Words.
Ravengate Press, 1989.